D0190174

Companion of God

The Wisdom and the Words of Dadi Janki

Companion of God

ISBN 1-886872-02-3

Published by the Brahma Kumaris World Spiritual University,
Literature Department, 65 Pound Lane, London NW10 2HH UK

There are Brahma Kumaris Centres in over 62 countries worldwide

Copyright 1996 Brahma Kumaris World Spiritual University
65 Pound Lane, London, NW10 2HH UK.

Printed by Waterside Litho, Chesham UK

This book has been produced by the Brahma Kumaris World Spiritual University,
a non-profit organisation, with the aim of sharing information as a service for the
spiritual growth of individuals.

No part of this publication may be reproduced, stored in a retrieval system, or transmitted, in any form
or by any means, manual, electronic, mechanical, photocopying, recording, or otherwise without the
prior written permission of the copyright owner. All rights reserved.

If one were to ask Dadi Janki the question, "how did you acquire such wisdom and was it personal research, divine intuition, or lessons learnt from life?", Dadi's answer would probably be to point her finger up above to indicate that the knowledge she shares has come from one Source. Interrogating her further, she would reveal that gurus, scriptures and devotion have not provided her with answers to the questions in her mind, but that her understanding has come from the knowledge revealed by the Supreme through the physical instrument of Prajapita Brahma the founder of the BKWSU.

Dadi remembers her experience of deep love for God from the age of 2 years. Her search for Truth began at the age of 11, and continued until she saw Brahma Baba after his own dramatic transformation. As a girl, she had known Brahma Baba since he studied and discussed the esoteric secrets of the scriptures with her uncles and relatives. At the age of 19, walking in a park she met Baba again. An intense bright light emanated from this person and Dadi was transfixed and knew instinctively that something divine and magical had transformed this man. From that moment, Brahma Baba became the instrument to share God's Truth, in words, vibrations and actions.

Over the past 60 years, Dadi's own relationship with God has deepened to the point of constant awareness through the inspiration and guidance of Brahma Baba. Often in challenging situations, Dadi would ask herself - "how would Baba deal with this?" and the image and activity of Brahma Baba would help her resolve the problem.

Today, Dadi is motivated by the desire to bring souls to God and share the enthusiasm and energy which she gives this task, as coming from the example of Brahma Baba. It was Brahma Baba's total surrender and obedience to God, his humility, generosity of spirit and purity of heart which are the guiding principles for Dadi and the students of the BKWSU even now.

To BapDada

*We thank you for this
original and
beautifully polished
'jewel' and all the
jewels of wisdom she
has given to
all of us.*

CONTENTS

CONTENTS

INTRODUCTION

This book is long overdue, probably by several decades. In many ways it is quite remarkable that Dadi Janki has not yet been discovered by the world at large for her wisdom and her achievements.

Achievement is all too often measured by position, power and possession, normally acquired through the process of accumulation. Dadi's achievements are acquisitions of a different dimension: through renunciation. For the past sixty years, it has been Dadi's daily practice to take up her position as close as possible to God for a personal conversation and silent counselling. She now finds herself as the Joint Administrative Head of the internationally expanding Brahma Kumaris World Spiritual University. Not bad for someone with no formal education.

Dadi will never profess to having any possessions, apart from the virtues of her own soul, and even these she will attribute to God. Yet, when her life is examined on a material level, she has been instrumental for a number of tangible miracles. When she arrived in London in 1974 she shared a small two bedroom flat in Kilburn. This was to be the first Brahma Kumaris centre outside India. During the decade of the eighties the number of regular students in London built up to several hundred. They would begin each day in a run-down and damp community centre in Dudden Hill. This was the time of renunciation, led by Dadi, which provided many lessons and inspirations for us all. By 1991 it had also enabled the building of Global Co-operation House, the University's new International Centre in north west London. In 1993, a Palladian stately home outside Oxford was purchased to become the Global Retreat Centre. And more recently, in 1995, Dadi inspired and oversaw the acquisition of the property in Regent Street which is now the Brahma Kumaris Information Centre.

Each of these, and numerous others around the world, are monuments to decades of selfless service and the shedding of ego. They are evidence of how the universe will rush to the aid of one whose sincere wishes and inspirations are for the spiritual upliftment of those who seek to improve themselves and know God.

For the past two decades, at the invitation of the students and teachers of the university in over sixty countries, Dadi Janki has repeatedly toured the world. Each morning she speaks at the centre she is visiting, including several days a week at Global Co-operation House, her base in London. In the evenings she gives lectures at public programmes and special tuition to the University's teachers.

It seems inevitable that at any moment now this remarkable woman will become well known to the world. May this book in some way be a step towards achieving that. Many heads and hands have been given with immense love to this, the first published compilation of Dadi Janki's words from her classes and lectures over the past ten years. While praise is not necessary, acknowledgment is important. Deirdrie O'Toole trawled hundreds of lectures and classes to compile extracts on a variety of topics. Sharonah Stillerman translated Dadi's words into crystal clear, powerful and essenceful language. Carol Rickard and Mary Newton gave their always gentle hands and intellects to editing and shaping the direction of the book. Jillian Sawers and Liz Corrigan processed many of the words and patient proofing was by Lynn Henshall and Joy Genese. Marisa Jacobs designed the simple and elegant graphics on each page, all contributing to the result you see before you now.

Welcome to the mind and the heart of Dadi Janki. We are sure you will derive much pleasure as you dip into these enchanting and powerful pages, whenever you wish to meet this living master of spirituality and close companion of God.

Dadi Janki

PROFILE

Dadi Janki is a woman of wisdom... A woman who, through understanding spiritual truths, has reached a position of personal peace and power. In a world which is teetering on the edge of 'extreme' chaos, Dadi Janki has discovered her own personal world of balance and order.

At 80 years of age, Dadi Janki is internationally acknowledged as a great teacher and mentor and continues to offer inspiration to many people who are searching for peace and harmony in their heart and in their homeland.

As Joint Administrative Head of the Brahma Kumaris World Spiritual University (BKWSU), Dadi Janki provides a working leadership model for all women and men who are seeking to integrate both male and female qualities into their personal and professional lives. Dadi lovingly engages people of all faiths and walks of life to be true to their spiritual self; to undertake their unique and individual part in the play of creating the future - a world worthy of the generations to come. In short, Dadi Janki calls us all to our potential.

"What kind of world is forming now, beyond this winter of war and sorrow, of poverty, pollution and death? In the winter, we foresee the spring. Those with a positive vision of the future give us an image of a world on this planet where all things are given freely, where the highest human potential is fully realised. But we can get to that stage only when there are leaders to take us there."

Dadi Janki

Acknowledgement of Dadi's work came in 1992 when she was invited to be one of the ten Keepers of Wisdom, an eminent group of world spiritual leaders convened to advise the Earth Summit in Brazil on the fundamental spiritual dilemmas which underpin current worldwide environment issues.

Over the past 57 years, Dadi Janki has dedicated her life to the service of humanity. She began her spiritual apprenticeship in 1937 at the age of 21 and was one of the founding members of the BKWSU. She spent 14 years in an enclosed community where intense meditation practices and the study of spiritual knowledge provided her with a firm foundation for the future. Dadi's purest wish is that all people find the inherent truth of their own spirituality and, as such, realise the potential of their personal relationship with God, the Supreme Soul. In essence, this is the foundation of her lifelong work.

Through the BKWSU which Dadi co-administers, the ancient Eastern principles of Raja Yoga are taught. The fulcrum of Raja Yoga is a silent form of meditation which over the past twenty three years has provided many interested people outside India with an opportunity to understand and appreciate more deeply their values, their vision for themselves, their future and their faith. Dadi Janki has been instrumental in bringing and translating this valuable self management philosophy from the mystic realm of India to the hard nosed, practical arena of our modern world.

Most of all, Dadi Janki is a visionary whose uniqueness lies in her unswerving optimism and a heart which is rich with compassion. She is a soul who refuses to set limits and boundaries as to what is achievable and in so doing inspires others to believe that they too can make the impossible possible.

A WOMAN OF WISDOM
AND A TEACHER OF TEACHERS

by Sister Jayanti

Is it possible for a mortal to make God their constant friend? Dadi Janki has demonstrated that it is possible to have a living relationship filled with spirituality. This perhaps has been Dadi's greatest contribution to the lives of thousands of people - to transform the image of God from a distant figure of fear and awe to a loving Parent and Wise Teacher who cares, supports, nurtures and uplifts each one. She can be described perhaps as an electrician - one who can repair the broken links, reconnect the wires of the soul with the Supreme Source of Light and Might, the Powerhouse who is God.

With humility, and a heart so clear that it sees only the goodness of each human being, Dadi has absorbed Truth from God so deeply that each breath and each moment is filled with that wisdom. Destiny brought me into contact with Dadi at the age of 8. As a child, the dominant memories are of Dadi's love and generous heart - constantly sharing physical and spiritual gifts. Dadi's stability and consistent yogi life were a reference point during my adolescent years of turbulent change. At the time when I was ready to listen, Dadi shared insights that opened up the closed doors of perception.

Events brought Dadi and myself to London together in April 1974. Living with Dadi day and night has been an incredible fortune that empowered the soul to learn, stretch, grow and evolve. I have observed Dadi playing with the jewels of spiritual knowledge and sharing them at each moment. Dadi is never too tired or too busy, it's never too late. She keeps her personal channel always clear and open so that God's light and love constantly fill her. She then manages to step out of the way, so that this light and love flow across to each one who enters her sphere of

contact. Being a translator for Dadi for several years has been a unique education and training. I would be 'the fly on the wall' - observing souls come in distress and leave dancing with joy. Souls coming with confusion and, Dadi enabling them to see facets that they couldn't perceive alone, leaving with clarity and strength. Each day Dadi would deal with hundreds, sometimes thousands, of people and she would give each one regard and listen to them with respect. Sometimes her patience would be challenged, sometimes her trust, but Dadi has not yet ever lost hope for souls or let go of her trust in them. She recognises their qualities more clearly than they themselves know and awakens them to fulfil their potential. It was with good reason that the Founder, Brahma Baba, entrusted her with the role of being the Teacher of Teachers.

Dadi's power of communication extends far beyond the words she uses. It is a fact that each word spoken comes from the depth of her experience and application. However it is her experiments with the power of silence that have the greatest impact. The power of silence filled with God's love and joy has visibly changed the attitudes of people. The depth of stillness emanating from her presence has answered many questions. The power of silence has made visions and dreams a practical reality, dissolving many obstacles that come in the way.

Dadi Janki demonstrates the method of transcending all limits - age, health, gender, personality and nature - to live in the canopy of God's love and share that protection with all.

Sister Jayanti is the Director of the Brahma Kumaris in London

Inspiration

How can we serve those around us?
By making our lives inspirational and
interacting with tact and wisdom.
Even if there isn't the chance for actual
conversation we can learn to take in each other's presence
in a positive way,
homing in on their goodness
and making their specialities our own.
This creates an atmosphere of love and regard,
which makes it easy then to
share spiritual experiences.
We should be so cheerful,
and our lives such examples,
that they say,
'Here is an angel.'

Faith
in Others

If there is a need to take responsibility for something, then of course, you should. However, if a situation is not your business, or someone else is in charge, then don't get caught up in it. If you want to help, you can still involve yourself in a more subtle way through faith.

Faith in others does a lot of work. It doesn't mean blind faith - observing helplessly while keeping your fingers crossed - it means to remain alert to what's going on, and then to fill another with the strength of your faith to such an extent that they feel able to do whatever needs to be done. This means having faith, but also donating the power of your faith. If the other person is honest and truthful, your faith will work for them. In this way, we can learn to truly help each other.

Problem Solving

The trick to problem-solving is to get at the root of a problem before
it even shows up.

This requires virtues such as objectivity, clarity and honesty, because the
solution to all problems is Truth. Truth means your spirituality, that is
essence, the way something is before attitudes and opinions are added.
This truth will bring you closer to God, and His pure influence will
allow you to perceive the essence of any problem, easily. Working on a
problem at the level of its essence is a beautiful experience. This beauty
has a transformative effect, not just on you and the problem, but on
those who cause them, too.

Every day you should ask yourself how much you have thought of
yourself in your essenceful form, that is, as a spiritual being, an eternal
child of the Divine. This is the method to increase not just your
awareness, but your spiritual beauty as well.
This makes problem-solving easy.

Knowing God

How do you know when you have recognised God as He really is?

The main sign is
You start to become like Him:

You take everything from its intrinsic, spiritual perspective;
You see and interact with everyone
on the basis of your spiritual identity and theirs
You are imperturbable, with a sense of values
that is never undermined

True recognition of God
- who He is and what He gives -
makes you feel as if you belong to Him and He to you
All He has becomes yours

Relationships

When a relationship is not working, it is usually because there are needs
and expectations that are not being met. There might be so much anger
or hatred that your only desire might be just to run away from it all.
However, this is not a solution! It merely reflects your lack of
understanding about where the real problem lies.

The root of all needs and expectations is an unfulfilled spiritual desire.
Satisfy your spiritual desires through the practice of
meditation and you'll be able to interact successfully with anyone.
No longer needy, you will enter into relationships simply to share and
enjoy. There'll be no strings attached in the way you give of yourself;
your love will be unconditional.

We must learn to bring spirituality into our relationships.
Others will learn by our example.
It's a way of inspiring and uplifting each other.

The Spiritual Path

A spiritual path is like a school. Not a regular school where you learn
ordinary skills, but a spiritual school where you learn the skills of spirit:
like how to remove flaws in your character, or how to remain unaffected
by the negative influences around you.

Some people think that if they follow a spiritual path, they won't be able
to cultivate their individual talents. However, what kinds of talent do
people really need nowadays? To remove one's own ego is a great talent;
to love others is another. There is no need to study all those other
complicated things. If you have the nature of following God, then God's
nature will become your own. Become true; reveal your true self
through your spiritual study, and claim a spiritual degree!

The Spiritual Army

Against the forces of falsehood and evil, the spiritual army is now being shaped. The forces of evil are all forms of negativity. What do you have to do in order to be a good spiritual soldier? First of all, don't be afraid. Although these forces of negativity are within the self as well as in the world, faith in your ultimate victory will give you the strength to face all challenges. Secondly, pay attention to becoming virtuous, not just to remaining peaceful. Also, stay alert. Alertness is probably the most important characteristic of a successful warrior. Everything within an army depends on alertness - promotion, progress, victory and defeat. If a soldier is not alert, he'll be dismissed. Spiritual alertness will help you to recognise negativity as soon as it comes up. Finally, if even only one soul remains alert, there is then safety for many others.

Trust

Trust is essential if you want to help people.
There are two kinds of trust - trusting others and getting others to trust
you. People will naturally start trusting you when they see you
overcoming problems in a reliable and constant way. However, a more
powerful and long-term way of gaining people's trust is to give them the
experience of your trust in them.

This is an art which can be cultivated by the following:
never listen to gossip and never foster it yourself; form neither
judgments nor opinions; rather, be spiritual and clean in your
feelings. Learn to develop good wishes for others. This will be the
ultimate measure of your ability to trust.

Connection
with God

The connection with God is automatic for those who have faith.
By faith I mean faith in life as in the expression,
"Whatever has happened is good,
Whatever is going to happen will be even better"

To develop faith, let go of your arrogance and make your intellect clean
Don't let yourself be influenced by anyone

Listen to God with the consciousness of being His child
Don't listen carelessly
Listen attentively, with love and self surrender
Then, when thinking or simply talking to yourself
keep in mind what God has said

The deeper your connection with God
the more power you receive
Fear finishes,
Everything in your life begins to feel easy
You become clean, sensible, and good

Calming
the Mind

Don't give your mind permission to get disturbed
A disturbed mind is easily influenced
This will cost you your peace
Learn to maintain your peace
by freeing yourself from attachments

Competing or comparing yourself with others
will not allow you to focus inwards
An inner focus allows you to
keep your eye on your higher self
Remember your original nature
It allows you to forge a link with the Divine
Then it becomes easy to recognise useless thoughts
and replace them with a spiritual perspective

Introversion replaces inner sorrow
with praise for God
You feel delight. You feel renewed.

God is teaching us how to turn within
so listen very carefully.

Keep a check on yourself and change
Don't wait for others to say something.

A calm mind is not just peaceful
It is focused, Self-Directing and Divine.

Purity

A powerful, yet often misunderstood, aim of spiritual study is purity. Purity of the soul means a return to its original divine qualities. The soul has become so polluted with less than divine qualities, it can hardly enjoy being alive. Purifying the soul puts the higher self back in charge - useless and negative thoughts are removed and annoying habits finish. A pure soul cannot be touched by sorrow; indeed the power of purity is such, it serves to remove the sorrow of the whole world. Purity restores happiness - even bliss.

All you need to do, in order to re-establish your purity, is want it. But you need to want it intensely, to the exclusion of everything else. The one thought, "I must become completely pure", sparks a fire of love between you and God. This fire melts away all the pollution, and your purity becomes such a power that it frees you from all battles for ever, making you a true and eternal companion of God.

Friends and Relations

If my friends and relations do not choose to accompany me on my
spiritual path, why should I chase after them trying to get them to
change? They won't listen to me anyway, no matter what I say.
A better approach is to focus on my own change process. A river doesn't
need to urge people into drinking its water. People are naturally drawn
to it, provided its waters are pure, free-flowing and sweet. In the same
way, become so attractive through your spiritual efforts, everyone will
want to join you, naturally.

We are hindered in this by attachments, which tend to make us forget
that our well-being is not dependent on others at all, that we each have
the capacity to flow and sparkle in our own unique way. Having
forgotten this we developed the habit of turning to others to
feel good about ourselves. Using other people in this way is a deceptive
source of well-being, and this deception leads to a great deal of pain. We
can change this habit by keeping an eye on our aim. If we don't, our
spiritual powers will be destroyed again and again as we allow ourselves
to come under the influence of limited emotions. Instead of losing out
like this, we should pay more attention to what we are doing. We will
only be able to make others free, when we free ourselves first.

Wisdom of
Tolerance

Tolerance is based on going beyond the superficial things that divide us. It's the result of turning within and coming to know the Self. If I can deal with my own ego, then my own anger can be resolved. This goes a long way in resolving external issues too. With my own ego out of the way, I will be able to handle anything! Otherwise, it's just the same old thing - you versus me, yours versus mine etc - intolerance. If I'm unselfish and honest in my heart, I am concerned about others' needs, and am full enough to give. When you know the self in this way, then you can know others. "I should be understood" changes to "I should understand." Not, "They should change", but "I will give what's needed." Patience, peace and maturity develop. Spiritual tolerance cultivates innate wisdom, the kind you can't get from books.

Turn within and in silence fill yourself with your Godly inheritance. Always remember, you don't have to prove anything. Whatever is true is going to be revealed, anyway. Working to win the hearts of others is what will bring happiness to your life.

Obstacles on the Path

Obstacles are inevitable

So don't get upset

Any form of worry erodes your strength

Never see a situation as difficult

Never ask, "Why has this happened?"

Never feel you're on your own

Remember

God is always with you

God is giving you support

Take time to go into Silence

Silence stops confusion

Your power will be restored

Many obstacles occur because of your own mistakes

Don't become someone else's obstacle

because of your own

Giving your
Heart to One

One task of those of us on a spiritual path is to help others
experience belonging to God. This means helping them identify with
their spiritual personality.

I shall be able to do that only when I have effected this
transformation myself. The challenge in this comes in two
varieties: the influences of those around me and the more subtle
influences from deep within my own self. The former are easier to deal
with, because their potential for causing me pain is usually clear and
visible. The latter (ego for example) take more time because they are
subtle, thus harder to recognise and face.

When I give my heart to God alone, there is nothing but joy.
Giving it to humans can create joy but also sorrow, because my original
feelings of elevated, spiritual love for all are reduced to the limited.
The feeling of universal love is replaced by an attraction to only some.
This is not a basis for constant joy.

When I subject myself again and again to limited emotions, my spiritual
personality suffers. It is a most subtle form of dishonesty, as I am
not supposed to be an example of the limited but, rather, a model of
the Divine. My aim is not to make others like me, but to make
them like God.

Making Peace

There is something that you can do to help create peace in the world, and that is to make yourself peaceful. The first step in this is an interest in doing some real soul-searching to find out what has made you peaceless in the first place. By turning your mind within, you discover, underneath the many surfaced emotions of everyday life, a deep, undisturbed pool of spiritual well-being. You need to explore that part of the self, not just to understand it, but to experience it, again and again. This is a very satisfying experience, one that refreshes the soul and fills it with peace. From this vantage point, it becomes easy to recognise the kind of thoughts and feelings which are self destructive. The power of self-realisation will work wonders in transforming these destructive mental habits. You will stop blaming others for your peacelessness, and get on with the work of cultivating your truth.

Peace is made up of many things: love, patience, wisdom. You should not be content with just a little of it, but fill yourself completely. As you practise putting these into your interactions with others, your very nature will become peaceful. This proves to be of benefit not only to yourself, but to all those around you as well. Thus you are becoming a helper in world transformation. It isn't enough for you simply to be peaceful. You must spread the waves and create an atmosphere of peace through your thoughts, words and interactions with others.

Our's is a peaceless world. Only when you truly adopt your original religion of peace, can you hope to bring peace to the world.

27

Spiritual Progress

There is benefit for you in every situation. If, that is, you know
how to look for it.

The idea behind steady spiritual progress is to see every
circumstance and situation (particularly those that challenge you)
as a tailor-made lesson in your personal plan for self-development.

For example, in a situation where hurtful or angry words were
exchanged, why not see it as the chance either to perceive things about
your own character which need changing or to rehearse some virtue or
quality that you need to put into practice more often? Actually, we
should be grateful for the opportunity to evaluate ourselves.

In this way you can transform anything into a constructive lesson.
Never think that you've learned enough and now can stop. You should
love it when people try to correct you or give you advice. It keeps you
alert and gives you plenty of opportunity to put your truth into practice.
It's a sign of great danger to be unable to accept criticism and instead use
your understanding to criticise others. Realise deeply the significance of
every moment, and your spiritual progress will be assured.

Love & Relationships

The Virtue of Honesty

Love is connected to virtues. Virtues create love both within the self and within others. When virtues reduce, the quality of love also reduces. When all virtues are present, there is complete and pure love.

Out of all the virtues, the main one is honesty. If we don't feel someone is being honest with us, our love breaks. Whether it be my mother, father, husband, wife or friend, if we feel that they are being dishonest, love breaks.

In terms of our relationship with God, if we are honest with God we will draw His love. If we are not, that love will break. Even if we have no other virtue than this one of honesty, we will be able to draw God's love.

So see the importance of being honest.

Honesty with Myself

The first kind of honesty is honesty with myself. If I am
honest with myself, there need be no situation in which I am not honest
with others.

If someone does not believe me, if someone distrusts my
honesty, perhaps it is a sign that I need to become more
honest. Instead of blaming them, I should realise this, and look at how
to become more honest.

Honesty and Clarity

Honesty does not mean simply speaking your mind. Honesty means to
be very clear about everything going on inside you.
Where there is honesty, feelings become pure and clean.
Honesty is where there are no other thoughts or feelings inside,
other than those that God Himself would have.

Such clarity is reflected in your words; they will be filled with the power
of truth, and spoken with ease and without hesitation.
The genuine honesty cultivated within you is what will reach out
and touch others.

Superficial Love

Being easily influenced by people will diminish your ability to remain honest. Others will not be able to get that feeling of truth from you, and your interactions will not carry a feeling of love. They will seem superficial. Although superficial love is better than no love at all - at least it ensures that you don't become completely dry - it will nonetheless be obvious that it is not the real thing.

Love and Detachment

God is teaching us the art of loving. He is the Bestower, He is the
Ocean of Love and He is willing to give us so much. But first I have
to learn the art of detachment, otherwise I won't have the right
to claim His love.

Detachment is a talent as well as an art. It is developed through soul
consciousness which, together with a deep relationship with God,
will keep me from being deceived by the attraction of limited love.
It means to be so centred in the consciousness of my true spiritual
nature that there is a natural, automatic rejection of adverse
personality traits within me and illusionary attractions around me.
Detachment allows me to be unaffected by these and so able to
continue cultivating the values and virtues of my
spiritual personality.

God is willing to give us all His love, but if the first condition of
detachment is not met we will not be able to receive it. Turning my
eye in any other direction will block the truth and finish my
progress. It's a very strong pre-requisite.

The Ocean of Love

Until we learn how to detach ourselves from a limited consciousness, human love, with all its limitations, will attract us against our will again and again. Detachment of this sort is cultivated by reaching for God in such a way that we feel Him satisfying the needs of any and all relationships. God is the Ocean of Love, so it is possible to experience Him as our perfect father, mother, beloved, and so on, all at the same time. It is only when we expose ourselves to all the aspects of God's love that we are then purified, that is, made full by its power. A limited consciousness will not allow us to experience such fullness.

Only by being faithful to One can we fulfil ourselves in this way. Souls have the habit of being distracted by the physical world. We have to study and look after ourselves to ensure that this does not happen to us. The only thing that will break this habit is the practice of soul consciousness. By being introverted, by turning our attention to One, we will continue to receive light and might from God.

The Love of God

People tend to gravitate towards whatever produces an experience of love. They are drawn in that direction and often get stuck there. They form an attachment and this continues to suck them in. I was never attracted towards anyone or anything in this way. And I have always rejected the kind of love that some people offer after conferring some status or title.

I don't think I have ever run after anyone's love - not even at the point of my greatest spiritual search. I never expected it from my father, my mother, my husband, my guru, or my friends; from anyone. I always did have, however, a very deep desire to experience the love of God.

People started prayer and worship in the hope of receiving something from God; they had a pull, or desire, to experience the love of God.

Perfect Love

The experience of perfect love is deep within our
subconscious personality and, because we had this experience at
some point, we have been searching for it ever since. It is exactly
because of this deep inner experience that we will always be
dissatisfied with any kind of false love.

Although false love might work for a little while, ultimately we will
always feel that something is missing and that what we are
experiencing is not true, real love. So the search is
then taken up once again.

Our search for perfect love eventually pulls us back to finding and
experiencing the love of God.

Love for Study

When we embark upon a spiritual path, we automatically receive a
lot of love from God in order to have the power to free ourselves
from other limited supports. We are like little babies who don't need
to do anything in order to receive that love. But then, as we
continue on the path, growing older and stronger, God wants to
teach us how to use our own head. So He stands back and
watches: is the child following His teachings properly, is the child
observing spiritual principles? He watches to see whether we
study well and change, or whether we become lazy or careless
in the study.

If I am not studying properly, I lose my right to that love.
The love will be there, but I will no longer be able to connect to it.
If I don't study properly - if there has been no integration of
spiritual understandings into my everyday, practical life - how much
further will I be able to go? I won't be making my life good, so what
goodness will I have to share with others? How can I be an
inspiration to make the lives of others good? God gives special love
to those children who are ready to help Him in His special task.
If I don't study how can God give me that love?

Surrender to God's Love

Learning the art of true, Godly love is a feature of
transcendence. It is like ascending to the very peak of a
mountain. At the bottom, at the beginning of the journey, it doesn't
matter so much if you misplace your footing and slip - it won't be
that dangerous. But the higher you go, the more narrow the path is.
If you slip while higher up, you will hurt yourself an hundredfold.

If you find that the laws governing your spiritual progress are too
strict, this can only be because you have not yet
understood nor truly experienced God's love. People do not
surrender themselves to God on the basis of spiritual
knowledge, but rather because of their attraction to God's love.
They experience the honesty in His love, and this makes them
believe that their life here and now can become honest and good.
Understanding comes later, the laws come later.
The first experience is love.

For this to happen, simply allow yourself to be the child again.
God is happy to take you into His lap with the
unlimited, unconditional love of the perfect Parent.

Courage

I need Courage
to remain true to myself in today's artificial world
This is not a small thing

However,
The very purpose of a spiritual study is
to restore Courage
The Courage to stand for what I believe in

My original, true nature is of peace and divinity
To experience this is to be convinced
of the absolute value of my intrinsic worth
I can face any opposition
with the strength of my convictions

Many people have difficulty believing in their higher self
Others simply no longer believe in the future

Self-realisation removes doubts
My original nature is peace
I am not a slave to my personality traits
(I am their creator)
I am a spectator as well as an actor in the Drama of life
Whatever is happening is beneficial

As I incorporate these truths into my life
my courage will never fail me

Child
of God

Do you know yourself as a child of God?

Or are you so overwhelmed by the circumstances of life
that you feel you have no time to be with God?
"There are too many things I have to do," you say
This is a perfect example of attachment - to the features of your life,
not to mention your own ego as well

As an actor on the stage of life
You need to detach yourself from the roles you are playing and
Get in touch with the part of you that
is not an act.

The one experience of 'being' which is not a role, not an act, is
'being the child of God'

I am, I have always been and I will always be
God's child
Never doubt this

There is such strength in this experience
You will easily rise above adversity
Sorrow will finish and your heart will dance.

Belonging to God fills you
with the innocence of a child and the wisdom of God.

Original Peace

It is not necessary to search for peace.

It is within.

Your original state is one of peace.

External situations will pull you away from your peace.

If, that is, you let them. Internal feelings can also pull you away.

Tiredness, for example, leads to irritability.

Learn to be in charge of yourself and maintain your peace:

centre your awareness on your spiritual form -

a tiny star-like point of light,

seated in the middle of your forehead.

Really experience the difference between You the Sparkling Star,

and your body, the physical vehicle.

Learn to detach yourself from the vehicle.

Even a few moments of this practice, if done regularly,

will return you to your natural state of peace.

Tiredness will vanish. Irritability, too.

And your actions will be filled with love - for the self and others.

Friendship

Friendships on the spiritual path require caution, if we're to enjoy them fully. Sometimes we get so involved in our relationships, that our own individual spiritual progress is undermined. This is a mistake, because the very purpose of friendship is to uplift, and if I am remiss in my spiritual efforts, I will not be able to exert the positive influence of my own most elevated state.

One should always maintain the intention of being of help to friends. But that help needs to be pure, that is without any desire for praise, and above any reactions of ill-feelings or sorrow. Offering this kind of help will only further my spiritual growth.

If, on the other hand, my offer is tainted, 99% of its sweetness will be removed, and people will notice this. In fact, it's the sweetness which creates spiritual friendships, the willingness to listen and learn from each other, in order to grow.

Comparison with Others

Comparing your progress in self-development with that of others will leave you vulnerable on three counts: you'll either feel inferior, superior, or impressed. All three of these states are dangerous because they all disregard the underlying principle of our true connection with each other - mutual love and regard, based on independently generated self-esteem.

To protect yourself from this vulnerability, make sure that your attention remains turned within, towards the spiritual experience of pure pride. Staying centred in your elevated self-respect will help you remain undisturbed by others around you. Keep asking yourself, "Who am I?" "How would my spiritual personality respond to this event or person?" This will help to centre you further, and allow you to enjoy the successful efforts of others.

Emotional Pain

In a situation of emotional distress, you usually have two options: to face
the problem, or not. Processing a problem means you are facing it.
Suppressing the problem means you are not.
There's a big difference between the two.

Processing is to the mind what digesting is to the stomach. If your
digestive system can't handle certain foods, you have to stop eating
them, otherwise you become sick. Similarly, if you find yourself in a
situation where you can't cope, don't just sit there taking it all in.
It's better to say something right there and then. To hold things inside
will not allow you to have a healthy mind.
What you take in will be indigestible and it will be obvious
to others that you are having a problem.

Our ability to cope is hampered by thinking too much about other
people. This causes problems in the mental digestive
system. The best mental 'antacid' is in-depth spiritual study.
This, plus a regular practice of self-awareness, penetrates the mind very
deeply, dislodging emotional pain at its roots. Only then can
emotion be purified, refined, and ultimately transformed.

Spirituality

Spirituality is the art of balancing your responsibilities: to yourself, your family and to the whole world. The basis for this is a deep understanding of the self, God and the law of cause and effect (karma).

Knowing the self enables you to be detached from physical factors and their limitations. Knowing God enables you to create a deep link of love and draw into yourself all attributes, virtues and powers, from the Source. Understanding the deep philosophy of 'karma' motivates you to settle debts of the past and perform elevated actions now.

Anyone can fall victim to the suffering of a poor state of mind, ill-health, loss of wealth or unhappy relationships. Human life depends on these four factors and yet each of them has become so fragile and unreliable. God's power restores tolerance and the ability to face anything. An understanding of the deep philosophy of karma reveals how elevated thoughts, pure feelings and good actions can resolve all difficulties for the self and for the world.

Quality of Thoughts

An enlightened person understands
that there is nothing to be gained by thinking about others
Pure thoughts and feelings will do all the work
There's no need to think any further

The quality of your thoughts will affect your
spiritual endeavour, so keep checking them
If you don't then at some point your mode of thinking will
become quite ordinary, no longer spiritual
The sign of this is that your mind begins to race and you start reacting
sensitively to little things
You become vulnerable not just to the
opinions of others but even to your own (limited)
way of understanding

Thoughts can be your own best friend, or worst enemy
It's up to you

Detachment

You need power to remain free from the influence of others.
Detachment is this power. If you can't stay detached from
influences, you will not be able to keep your thoughts under
control. From there it will be a downward spiral until all trace of
inner well-being is lost.

The first step in detachment is to understand who you are as a spiritual
entity. This allows you to 'detach' yourself from your physical identity,
and its world of limited thoughts and feelings, and 'attach' instead to
your spiritual personality, the being of inner peace and power.

A normal day will be filled with challenges to this detachment.
On the one side will be your spiritual awareness, but on the other will
be the attraction towards human beings and the material world.
Detachment is not a question of becoming separate from the latter, but
of simply remaining conscious of yourself as a spiritual being whilst
being in the world and playing your part. Detachment simply means to
keep yourself centred in your spirituality.

The Benefit
of Sickness

Being sick is an opportunity to experience yourself in a new way.
Do you understand and accept this opportunity readily? Or are you
unable to take advantage of it, too distracted by the illness?
If that is the case, then you need to take a closer look at yourself, to see
where another kind of sickness might lie.

Just as the outward cure for sickness involves going to a hospital,
seeing a good doctor, getting a comfortable bed and eating healthy
food, the internal cure is the same. I need to go to the Soul World,
where the Supreme Doctor resides, rest in the comfortable bed
of His remembrance, and eat the nourishing food of pure
and positive thoughts.

Sickness is the chance to teach the mind to remain independent of the
physical state and so connect with your inner resources of peace and
silence. This is the ultimate cure.

God's Light

Many religions believe that God is Light. The wisdom of God is also Light. And those who study it become light, and easy!

Who made this Light? God, from His own state of eternal enlightenment. God, Being of Light, makes the world around Him light, chasing away the darkness of ignorance. Light spreads from God, through His studious children, into the whole world.
Others receive this Light when they see the practical proof of it in the lives of His effort-making children.

God gives His Light from above for this service. The ones who catch it and share it will be happy, no matter how little may be received in return from humans.

Mercy

God is known as the Ocean of Forgiveness
and an experience of His mercy makes you feel
that you have made a best friend for life.
Peace makes its home in your heart.

When you accept God's mercy for you,
your perspective on life changes.
It is God's merciful vision that allows you to see
your potential for perfection. Then it becomes your turn to be merciful
to yourself. Mercy for the self means striving to be
true to that image of perfection.

By drawing from God whatever power is needed,
we can become whatever we wish.

Respect
for Others

Respect for others is the result of spiritual awareness.

With spiritual awareness, I recognise the efforts of those around me to improve themselves. This encourages me to focus more on the potential and unique specialities of my companions, rather than on their faults. In fact, this is the method to help people to be free from their faults.

I can judge the quality of my spiritual awareness by seeing how much faith I have in the ultimate transformation of my companions. This faith and love is true respect.

God as my Everything

Do you realise the importance of having a relationship with God?

Having had numerous relationships with human beings over a long period of time, the soul has now become so depleted and tired that it is hardly able to remember its purpose, let alone achieve it.

Making God your friend will bring Him close but in fact it is important not to limit your experience of God to just one kind of relationship. Experience them all - God as your Mother, Father, Companion, Beloved, Teacher, Guru, Child. Each relationship brings so much sweetness. If any one of these is lacking, you will be forced to take that support from a human being. This is a mistake, because no human at this point in time can offer you such consistent and unconditional love. Don't content yourself with a mere intellectual understanding of these relationships. Go into their depths and open yourself to the tangible experience of each.

Love

If your companion is God, then, even if you are alone,
you will never feel lonely.

Happiness will be yours whether you are with other people or not.
God's love produces a variety of such magic. It enables us to
interact with love and co-operation; it makes us into sources of mutual
inspiration. With worldly love, there is sometimes the
concern that this is going to interfere with my career or studies.
But love for God only enhances your ability to perform,
on all levels.

Self-Respect

The basis of self-respect is the faith that God loves me. Through this experience, I will be able to start loving myself. By studying God's virtues and incorporating them in my daily life, faith in my own inherent worth is enhanced.

It is often difficult to experience self-respect, because my sense of self is usually based on external things - praise, status, income, and so on. As these fluctuate, so does my self-appreciation. One day I'll feel there's no one as good as me and the next I'll feel utterly worthless. Actually, self-respect is not a matter of what I am doing in my life, but rather the degree to which I bring quality and virtue to each act.

Silence

There is a part of you that is perfect and pure. It is untouched by the less than perfect characteristics you've acquired by living in a less than perfect world.

It is filled with divine qualities, so is in a constant state of resourcefulness and well-being. Its total absence of conflict and negativity of any sort makes this part of you a Still-Point; a deep, enriching experience of Silence.

Make time to practise reaching this inner place of Silence. It will bring you untold benefit.

First, it allows you to manage your thoughts better. You will find, for example, that there is no need to think as much as you do, that simply sitting in Silence will emerge, effortlessly, much of all that you need.

Second, the experience of Silence releases you from the grip of your negative programming and conditioning. You will more easily experience the truth of your inner peace and dignity. This further aids the mind in remaining focused and capable.

Third, the power of Silence can be shared. As you increase your experience of Silence, your power can help those without power to continue in their efforts of self-development and the experience of peace. Your stock of Silence plus an additional stock of true, powerful thoughts will help others go beyond the limited into the unlimited and the divine.

It feels so good to 'go beyond' in this way, to leave behind thought and speech and become quiet for a little while. It's so refreshing and nourishing; it's habit-forming. Love for spiritual introversion, solitude and silence complement our life in such a beautiful way.

Love and Relationships

Eliminating the Vices

We began to descend from our spiritual heights when we started using the body in the wrong way. We are souls, and we began the cycle of birth and rebirth through physical bodies. Eventually we began to use the body for vice and, from that time onwards, a lot of rubbish began to accumulate in the soul. This is how we lost our peace, happiness, love, purity. All the negative things, which have affected us in this lifetime and those gone by, have penetrated deeply within the soul. It is nothing ordinary to eliminate them all.

We start by eliminating the obvious vices; dependencies such as tobacco, alcohol, lust. But the real effort is in removing the subtle vices, like ego. The subtle vices do not allow us to feel we belong to God.

Developing Humility

The difficulty with ego is that it is deeply concealed. Most people don't even know they have it. Saying something to them about it just increases their arrogance.

Ego destroys love. It destroys the ability to learn, so there is no more give and take. I pass through many situations all day long and make sure I don't stop exchanging love. Ego can be overcome by developing humility. There should be as much humility in the soul as there is honesty so that the more honest I become, the greater the humility I have. Both go together. If I know how to bow, there will be love. If I don't know how to bow, love finishes. I have to bow down again and again. Bow, bow, bow.

The secret behind this is to never stop the give and take of love with God. In this way, I can make my heart very strong so that I am no longer hurt by anything. Hurt feelings are the main reason why the give and take of love stops.

Understanding

Most people don't understand themselves. There isn't the patience to
understand themselves or others. We need to make time for this.
We get too impatient. Very often, because we are not willing to take
this time, misunderstandings continue. We don't take the time to
listen to someone quietly and try to understand them. Then we start
inventing things about them, because we simply haven't taken the
time to understand.

Balance

To focus solely on yourself, without any concern for what is
happening to others, reflects a weakness in your effort. Cultivating
humility will allow souls to come close. From there you need to
balance maintaining a certain formality or quietness - so that
relationships don't become too casual and familiar, giving love
with ease and lightness.

Power and Love

Right now what the soul really needs most is power. Having been
through birth and rebirth, accumulating rubbish along the way, the
soul is burdened and depleted and therefore unable to perform to its
greatest potential. Power is gained, enabling us to stay with God and
reach the destination, when we use our inner resources in the right
way. Wasting the mind on ordinary, mundane, conditioned thinking
is a waste of time and energy. Souls leave the path, they leave God,
because they have wasted their thoughts, words and breath in this
way. Blaming others and complaining are just making excuses.
This is another mistake which wastes more energy and causes more
loss of power.

There isn't time to behave in this way any more. Understand that
you need power and start cultivating it.
As power develops, so will love.

Pure Feelings

People have experienced a lot of deception in their lives. There has been a lot of exchange of everything that is false, so feelings have been destroyed. It is why some people have stopped feeling altogether, and have rejected the world. However, when a soul starts receiving something from God, the heart opens up. So let us take God's love and have pure feelings. Let us experience what pure feelings are. Let us have trust in each other and faith in ourselves. Let us learn to love ourselves. Let us have purity in our feelings, then we can experience love. Let us take from God and give to others. When we have very powerful good wishes for others, good feelings for others, those feelings reach them. We can help each other through the power of our good feelings.

Deep in my heart there is just this one feeling: just as I have received so much from God, may all God's children receive the same from their Father.

Physical Pain

It is possible to experience so much love from God
that whatever pain you have, you will no longer feel it
Experience Him as the Mother and let Him soothe it away
in a second, as you sit on His lap

It's much better than crying
(which doesn't work anyway)
And also, it's a spiritual victory

Be tolerant with pain
It's trying to teach you something
Don't look at the illness, see the lesson instead.

Remembrance of God is the quality cure
Understand the relationship of happiness to pain
It's a magician, it makes it disappear

So detach yourself from the body
in the firm faith of God
And the pain will finish, very quickly

Accomplishment

Spiritual accomplishment means:
You are fully centred in your spiritual identity
You know yourself as a child of God
The present is fully experienced, the past completely finished
and the future clearly understood

Spiritual accomplishment is received from God

A distracted intellect will not be able to turn towards God,
and receive
It will be too busy thinking, "How?" and "Why?"
and turning to the world for understanding,
which only serves to divert the intellect, even more
It's a lack of faith
which destroys spiritual progress

So don't be distracted; rather,
Tolerate and persevere
And you'll be able to receive everything that God is giving

Subtle
Service

Your pure vibrations are a subtle form of service

Love, peace, joy, wisdom — these are pure vibrations
They are carried out into the world
through your thoughts and actions
wherever these are filled with the Divine

So make your every moment pure:
Understand the difference between the ordinary and the Divine
Then put the Divine alone
into practice
Remember that you are Master of both your mind and body
Then give your commands
and keep them in order
As you learn how to tell your mind what to do
Old ways of thinking and doing will change

As the Master of both your body and mind
You will see things not as they appear, but as they truly are
You react less, respond more

Your very presence becomes an invitation to truth
Your vibrations reach out, bringing coolness and peace
- words wouldn't be even half as effective -
The help is extended through your state of mind

And everyone is benefited, not just those around me
But all your brothers and sisters, the whole world over.

Staying Peaceful

I have faith that the force of Peace is
Greater than the atomic bomb
Greater than any power the world can produce

All of us need to put our faith in this force
Not, "I'll just keep my gun handy"
Or, "We'll just keep these bombs handy
...in case they're needed"
But, "I trust absolutely in this power"

I was once asked how I could stay so peaceful
trying to teach peace to so many different kinds of people

I just keep my aim in front of me:
To stay full of peace myself
Knowing this peace will reach my beloved ones
and, ultimately, the whole world

Traps

Keep yourself free from traps

Traps are:
Thoughts about others
Criticism of others
Criticism of the self
Doubts in the self
Etc., etc..

Exaggerating a problem
is also a trap

You can free yourself by:
Creating only pure thoughts
(about your eternal self, and others)
Cultivating good wishes
(whatever their behaviour towards you)
Maintaining God's remembrance
(to be able to remain true)

If somebody comes and insults you
especially in front of others (the Trap)
Just think, "This is a test"
and you will be free

Every thought, which keeps you Spiritual
- unable to take something personally -
will liberate you from all traps

Removing Unworthy Habits

First of all, don't be afraid of your sins
Because God will never stop loving you

He knows that love keeps a child growing
So just keep thinking of what He wants you to do
And do it

'Trying to do' will not work
'Trying' does not bring a reward
God's help comes only when there has been effort
from the heart
Having understood deeply
what you want to see changed

Sit with God and ask His forgiveness
He always gives it, anyway
Then share, ceaselessly, your experiences with others
This is a spiritual charity which settles accounts
Which is all that sin is, anyway

Then you'll begin to feel cleaner, lighter
and dear to God
The reminder to others that they can be, too

Cheerfulness

Inner cheer is destroyed by a conscience which bites
So learn to do everything in a worthwhile way
It's an art, which teaches you
to appreciate your inner beauty
(it makes you think twice about ruining it, too)

We used to be hard on ourselves when we made a mistake
It's much more effective to be handled with love
Telling the self off is a terrible habit
It subtly shapes a nature of sorrow

Finish the business of thinking of rubbish
And instead take delight in all that you've found

Talking to the Self

When you talk to yourself in your mind, which self do you address? And how? Usually people do not talk to their divinity, but to the most superficial aspects of their everyday personality. And often it's a stream of fears, complaints and a mindless repetition of old things. If we talked that way to another human being, we would have to apologise.

Learning to talk properly to the self is a spiritual endeavour. Thoughts from the past and worries about the future do not create good conversation. Instead learn to talk to your mind as if it were a child. Talk to it with love. If you just force a child to sit down, he won't. A good mother knows how to prompt her child into doing what she wants. Be a good mother to your mind, teach it good, positive thoughts so that when you tell it to sit quietly, it will.

Love your mind. Stay happy.

Ruler of
the Self

There is a connection between a mind which is peaceful and
behaviour which is good. It is interesting to note how the sensory
apparatus - sight, touch, hearing, taste and smell -
are involved in this.

For example, suppose I promise myself not to get angry any more,
because I've understood the harm it causes, but then later in the day I
'see' or 'hear' something negative. If I allow myself to forget my promise,
that is my level of awareness regresses to what it was, then my
immediate reaction will probably be equally negative. If, however,
I remember my promise, the same stimuli will most likely produce a
wiser, more resourceful response.

With spiritual study, my mind grows strong in its commitment to peace
and truth in action. This strength allows me to gain control over the
sense organs. I simply don't allow them to proceed as usual -
according to my conditioning. I remain consciously present, monitoring
whatever they do. It is the first step in becoming a Master -
ruler of the Kingdom of the Self.

Honesty

Spiritual honesty means, "To thine own self, be true." It is one of the pillars of greatness as it evokes a practical experience of God's love, and the feeling that God and I are very close. There is so much power in this experience. Unfortunately, instead of enjoying such greatness in a natural way, most people forego this opportunity by making excuses. Lying is the obvious form of dishonesty but, actually, making excuses is worse.

While falsehoods are usually noticeable, it can be a long time before I realise that I am making excuses. A lot of life can be wasted by this deception. When you think about it, whatever excuse could there be for not making yourself close to God?

Respect

We like to be shown respect, and many believe it is a right but, as in the case of most rights, there is a responsibility attached to it.
This responsibility needs to be understood in order for you to become worthy of respect.

True respect does not come from what we do, as much as how well we do it. This means that we are shown respect according to the virtues and qualities revealed through our behaviour.

Respect is not a matter of supply and demand.
On the contrary, if people pick up that you are even slightly in need of respect, they will usually turn away from you completely.

This is because the need to be respected indicates a gap somewhere in your sense of self - and most people are so busy trying to fill their own gaps, they get annoyed at the prospect of having to fill someone else's.

Be suspicious of any desire on your part for respect.
Indeed, such thoughts are a sure sign that no one is giving it to you anyway. The very act of trying to get respect from others proves you unworthy of it.

Fill yourself with Godliness.

Let Godliness be visible in your life. Godliness makes you worthy.

Don't be upset if you are shown disregard. Speak to a third party to check your behaviour. If you have done nothing wrong and your attitude is right, understand that the situation is a test of your ability to remain beyond the judgements of others.

Many such situations will come to test you. Understand them as a test of your self-respect. They are a test of your self-love and patience.

Fill all the gaps in your own sense of self by continuing to explore your true spiritual worth. As this awareness follows through into action, you will find it easy to respect others. When you are full, it is easy to make others full. When you are full, you pass all your tests. And passing all tests makes you worthy of the respect of others.

Spiritual
Health

Good spiritual health means I am free from diseases of the spirit

No traces of negativity remain

All obstacles have been overcome

My face sparkles with happiness

Good spiritual health comes from a healthy spiritual birth

Be born to your true self - the Personality of Purity -

by remembering God, your eternal Parent

I am living my life with God

I am talking to God

I am learning from God

Inner joy is the best of medicines

It all depends on what you hold in your heart

Spiritual Students

A good student on the spiritual path passes all subjects with honours. This means that spiritual understanding and power from God have been so well assimilated that not one of life's many challenges is faced without equanimity and truth. The heart is merciful and altruistic, never giving or taking sorrow. Feelings are pure; that is, devoid of any needs or expectations, and these pure feelings are shared abundantly with others. You will not achieve this by becoming a hermit and leaving everyday life; rather, you remain completely in the world, but at a distance from all its vice and negativity.

Now is the time to become such a successful student of life; you should never doubt yourself in this. Trust in God invokes His assistance. This plus your own determination will create the strength to progress. God will give you everything you need.

Love & Relationships

Looking for Love

Modern love has come out of the heart and gone into the head. This is why we have headaches, because the head instead of the heart has started to look for love. The poor heart has lost love and is unhappy. Whatever the age, young or old - even small children - everybody is looking for love.

Inside for Love

If you go inside yourself, there you will discover what love is. If you look for it externally, you will need to keep on looking because you will find only deception and sorrow. You have to go inside to look for love.

The Heart is Broken

People have lost faith in love. First there was the search to experience the unconditional love of God. When this was unsuccessful, faith in God was lost. As people then searched for love from each other, still without success, faith in love was lost.

There is a lot of misunderstanding about love. True love is not selfish love. The sign of selfish love is that a relationship will finish if you don't receive what you desire. Today there is selfishness within every kind of relationship - even within the relationship of mother and child or husband and wife. Selfish love always appears one thing on the outside, but is completely different on the inside.

Deception like this has made the heart very unhappy. Whatever love was there has turned to hate. When you end up feeling threatened by a relationship, unsure of where it is going to take you, your love will turn to hate. Many believe they have found true love only to discover later that they have been deceived.
Because there is no more honesty in the heart, the heart is broken.

Clean and Honest Heart

Deceptive love is love where there is no honesty in the heart. It
creates dependency, and looks more like a deal than a relationship.
This kind of love has become like a drug.

We don't want love that is going to make us dependent. Love should
be such that it makes honesty and truth grow. It is honesty that
shows us what love is and real love shows us what honesty is.

The way to free ourselves from dependency on false love is to
experience the fullness, the sweetness, of love that is true. Replace
poison with nectar and it will be easy to recognise the worthlessness
of false love. We should not just accept whatever love comes our
way - from here, there, everywhere. If somebody wants to give you
love, first see what kind of love they are offering. Your intuition
should realise very quickly what kind of love it is.

To experience true love we should ask: Is my heart clean? Is it
honest? Is it open? If it isn't, if my heart is still broken, I will not
be able to experience true love.

Arrogance

Some people don't want to have anything more to do with love. Because there has been deception from all sides, they have kicked love away. They think it is too complicated, too tiring. They say, "I'm not going to love anyone any more and I don't want anyone to love me, either." They don't even want to talk about it. They don't want to hear about motherly love, friendly love, any kind of love at all.

These are the ones who end up saying, "I just want to be independent." They think that love should mean freedom from all these things. Actually, this is a kind of arrogance. Such people do not understand that this earth is a field of action, and that this field and our being on it needs the water of love.

Life in the Jungle

Life without love is like life in the jungle. What is life like in the jungle? You are constantly afraid of what might come to you. You are isolated, not receiving any support from anywhere.

The First Act of Love

People don't know how to give love, nor do they know how to receive. Thus the heart is empty. This is why they don't know what love is. Actually, just to take the time and effort to understand what love is, is in itself an act of love.

True Love From You

True love is totally uninterested in that which is false. Superficial emotions which keep you on the surface of things are not the basis of true love. True love means pure love, and pure love is based on your innermost truth, goodness and desire to bring benefit to others. Being superficial and imagining things about others dilutes pure love. Being affected by other people's character also dilutes it. You need to endeavour to understand the things of pure love and to check that it is what you are working with.

Let your love be so true that even if others become your enemy, you do not stop loving them. You have to give love truthfully, from your heart. Your love should be such that you are able to place your hand on your heart and know that what you are giving is true. True love is what everyone wants, so this is what you should share.

True Love From God

God gives us true love. The key to being able to fill yourself with it is honesty. I have never hidden anything from God. I can't. He knows my heart very well and I know Him very well, too.

The virtue of remaining honest with God enables the soul to receive so much from Him. When there is true love in your heart for God, then in return you receive true love from God.

Kindness Always

The results of pure, true love are always positive. Those with pure love are never influenced by anyone. Their ability to discern never diminishes. When your love is pure, others will feel that your intentions are pure. There will be love in your vision. And there will be kindness in that love. In pure love there is always kindness.

Happy Heart and Cool Head

I have always been very cautious not to separate myself from God's
love, not to distance myself even in the slightest, thereby cutting
myself off from the experience of His love. I am also careful that my
intellect does not become engaged elsewhere, so that God can use it
whenever He wants. This is why my heart is always happy and my
head stays cool. I don't let just anything into my heart, which would
then require a lot of time and effort to remove. When I start
thinking about the past, present and future, old feelings stir in my
heart, all at the same time, and it takes a lot of hard work to remove
them. How could God give me love, how could I experience His
love, if I am always so busy in that?

No One Can Hurt Me

God's love actually changes me internally. Through God's love, everything old finishes. God's love makes me like a mirror - a mirror in which I can see myself clearly and through which others can see themselves - in no time at all.

The power of the love of God, the Almighty Authority, has accumulated in my soul. Because of God's love, my heart has become so strong that even if somebody does something to hurt me, I don't allow myself to get hurt. No matter what somebody might say, they cannot hurt me.

Love is Forever

The experience of God's love restores faith in God. However, for this faith to be powerful, it needs to be based not just on feelings and experiences but also on a clear understanding of the true nature of the self, God, and life. This makes the soul worthy and powerful. God gives us such deep, powerful love that this love becomes eternal. It is never destroyed, it can never be reduced.

Our love should remain eternal, too.

Parents of Love

When I first came to London, people used to ask if I were married,
and did I have any children? And I would say:
"Yes, I have one Husband, who loves me very much and who is very
good to me. He has freed me from this world of deception. He has
made me belong to Him. If there is anything in my heart, anything
that causes pain, He has so much love for me that He just erases it
from my heart. And so I have given Him a name: Dilaram, the One
Who Comforts My Heart. And I have two children: Patience and
Peace. So my life is very happy. Where there is patience and peace,
I can take and give a lot of love. Where there is no patience and no
peace, there is no love. Patience and peace are also the mother and
father of love. If I have patience, then my love for others will never
break quickly or easily, ever."

Desires

Desires are not the problem
Satisfying them is

God says: tell me all your desires and I will fulfil them
But people don't do this
They turn to others expecting someone else to fulfil them
Expectations are another kind of desire

Expecting to be praised, or recognised, or approved of
are the signs of little spiritual accomplishment
Over time, this will deplete you
Your work will turn superficial, for namesake only
and you will be distanced from the true blessings of others

God's pure desire is that we now become like Him
Our only desire should now be that, too

Knowledge

If I am a truly knowledgeable soul, I will be skilful in the things of
the spirit. I will be centred successfully in my spiritual identity.
I will be free from the influence of my past.
There will be only peace and happiness within.

True knowledge is not a question of intellectual understanding
alone. It is for incorporating in my daily life, in order to improve it.
My every thought, word and action becomes naturally aligned with
the laws of the universe.
All that has ever gone wrong begins to be put right.

This 'knowing' protects me from small-minded ways of seeing or
thinking of others. It enables me to feel love for everyone but
without losing energy by entering into a lot of matters with others.

This is the duty of those who have understood the self in depth.

Intellectual arrogance is the sign that I have not become truly
knowledgeable. True knowledge puts me in touch with the
sweetness of life and makes me equally sweet.

God
the Almighty

Why is God known as the 'Almighty'?
It is because He has 'All Might'
which He then offers to us children
in the form of an inheritance

He draws us to Him, filling us with power,
so that we can experience all aspects of truth

Through God's power
our minds become clean and refreshed
It is His power which takes us beyond the limited
into the experiences of the Divine

When we look at ourselves and at the world,
every step of positive change
is evidence of this Godly donation

My connection with God is revealed
through my character, relationships
and my general outlook on life

When I am feeling alone, or weak, it means
I am not letting God's power work for me
Being incapable of co-operation or loveful feelings also implies
that I am not experiencing the love of God

Why should I not begin to claim my inheritance, now?

Ethics

Ethics are a code of conduct which promotes virtue and character. There needs to be ethics in my personal, social and professional lives. To be ethical means to have a code of conduct for the self.

A personal code of conduct can be maintained when the intellect is not easily shaken by small matters. For this reason, it is useful to have self-discipline. Self-discipline makes everything accurate, beautiful, spiritual and simple.

It is easy to have good relations with somebody who has good self-discipline.

The first ethic and code of conduct is to have a generous heart. When your heart is not generous, there is distress; you can neither do what you want nor communicate clearly. You cannot even co-operate with others; feeling always low on energy, so cautious about how much you give. A generous heart is not a question of giving money, but a state of relating to everyone as an equal.

Integrity

Anybody who wants to be instrumental in serving the world needs to know how to work with integrity. Integrity elevates character and brings internal power. It reveals a pure attitude. Those with integrity maintain great humility, even while holding positions of high status and commanding a lot of respect. They do not alter their character or virtues according to whom they are with.
They have pride in themselves.

Integrity over a long period of time makes the soul powerful. The intellect is clear and does not mix truth with falsehood. A person with integrity is able to reveal truth through words spoken with wisdom. They never feel the need to prove truth. Because a clear conscience is the reward of such honesty, a person with integrity considers the consequences of every action and is never drawn mindlessly into anything. To behave in any lesser way is to deceive people.

Spiritual Education

A spiritual education teaches how to keep the mind free from tension and fluctuations. An unsteady mind is the result of letting yourself be strongly influenced by human situations. Spiritual awareness keeps you centred and thus protected. You claim increasing happiness and help others to do the same.

The world is a supermarket of sorrow. Don't buy any! A good spiritual education teaches you how to be discerning in your shopping. Refuse to accept anything but happiness from others as well as the world.

Contentment

First of all, understand discontentment. Discontent is caused
by a constant multiplication of desires

One desire leads to another until
there's never a moment when you feel fulfilled

Desires are like traps

Because of endless desires
Relationships have become very fragile
There is a lot of irritability and anger due to
selfish attachments (to possessions and people) and
pride (attachment to a particular image of the self)
Where there is discontentment, the heart can never be still
because wasteful, negative thoughts destroy peace

Contentment is the result of spiritual awareness,
which allows you to recognise negativity
It changes your pattern of thinking
As you tap your huge inner potential
all desires are fulfilled
And you regain your Peace

Understanding Sickness

A spiritual attitude towards sickness is to see it as a result of your own past actions. This is due to the law of karma, which states that whatever your situation is today, it is the result of what you have done yesterday. These actions may have been performed in the immediate past, or the far distant one. If you can accept responsibility in this way and your heart knows how to stay in the remembrance of God, then you will gain such power that even a major physical illness will not affect your ability to cope. Mountains are reduced to molehills. Without proper understanding the reverse is true and even a tiny physical complaint seems something enormous.

Spiritual understanding teaches you how to perform actions so as to guarantee yourself a healthy future. It makes you realise the importance of performing good actions as these result in a good future. For example, you can bring a lot of subtle energy and strength to yourself if you engage your body, mind and wealth in the service of humanity. An adverse affect, on the other hand, is produced when these same things are used in a negative way.

Learning

Some things facilitate learning, and other things destroy it

Arrogance destroys it
"I know this already"
Have this thought and learning will stop

Also, being tied up in a million things
Will not help you get to the depth of a thing
You can't really change until you get to the depth of a thing

When learning stops there is no more Change
There is no more Progress
And the soul, whose task it is to learn and change, is bereft

"This much I have understood, but tomorrow I will understand
even more." This thought is a thought of appreciation for what has
already been received.
It is a good way to ensure that more
will be received in the future

There will always be the opportunity to learn
for those who desire it

Learn in such a way so as to absorb the new and live it
That's being sensible, which is the aim of learning

Success

Success means to reach such a constant level of positive thoughts that
pure actions happen naturally. Pure actions are like good seeds which,
when planted, produce healthy, sweet fruit

"As you sow, so shall you reap"

Concern for the quality of my actions today
ensures the Success of my tomorrow

Virtues are the mainstay in this because
Success like this requires Hope
And Hope, in today's world, requires Courage
It is a matter of working from the strength of your convictions
Which is a spiritual kind of Honesty

Balance these qualities and your path will be easy
You will only move forward. Your Success will be assured

Courage alone does not bring Success
If there's only courage, there will be ego
It's courage plus honesty which brings God's help
and that is what guarantees the Success

"God is getting it done through me"
"I am simply an instrument in this task"
These are honest thoughts which elicit
God's help and protection

Humility is the result of such honesty and courage
A life of enthusiasm, courage, honesty and humility is inspirational
It's a way of helping others become Successful, too

Thought Power

Through our thoughts, we are either gaining power or losing it. With pure thoughts power is generated, and with impure thoughts power is destroyed.

Pure thoughts are those that express our spiritual personality. Impure thoughts are all the others. They have nothing to do with our truth. Thought is the vehicle which takes us from our non-spiritual self to our truth.

Spiritual knowledge is like a sieve through which we can filter out the untrue. Running our thoughts through it constantly ensures that we are heading in the right direction.

When thoughts are brought into action, they can be seen immediately.

When the mind is filled with virtues, they will be revealed in our actions.

By elevating our thoughts, we can literally end up purifying the self, inspiring others to do likewise. Our life in itself will be the inspiration for them to change. There won't even be the need to say anything.

Our vibrations of pure thought can reach out and touch the whole world. Our very life can do the work of a lighthouse.

Going Beyond

The effort you need to be making now is to come close to God.
To experience this, practise going beyond a limited consciousness of
yourself (body-consciousness) until eventually you can remain in a state
of constant, unlimited, spiritual awareness (soul-consciousness).
This is one of the most difficult things for any human being to achieve,
because we have incarnated in many bodies and have had so many
relationships. Connection with God makes it possible to remain
detached even whilst in the body and involved in human relationships.

In order to make such a connection with God, you must cut off all other
attachments. Yet they must be cut with love. Take help from God and
learn how to cut them yourself.

Happiness

There is no nourishment like Happiness
(it's an elixir)

There is no sickness like sorrow
(it's a poison)

Having been sorrowful for so long
the soul is now desperate for Peace

There can be no real Happiness until
the soul finds its Peace

Deep inner Peace,
the kind born of union with God,
gives so much power
You forget about sorrow completely
There's only gratitude in the heart
and so much Joy

The experience of true Happiness cures
the sickness of sorrow

This is a remedy
not just to create Happiness and Joy
in your own life
But for creating it in the world, too
A cheerful face goes a long way
towards making everything better!

Blessings from God

When you understand that you belong to God
then God is responsible for you
You are in His care

As love for God increases
Spiritual understanding wells up inside you
and there is so much power that
you feel: "There is nothing I cannot accomplish"

As God sees your love and faith
He gives MORE love and faith in return
And you feel: "My life is in His hands"

To receive God's blessings, simply
Remember all that He is giving
Keep it alive in your heart and
Be accountable

God's blessings go only to those who are honest

Women
as Servers

The idea of women playing any role outside the home was strongly opposed in the community where I grew up. That was a long time ago and things have changed. But I didn't wait for the change. I had the strong desire to work for the upliftment of humanity, and that's what I set out to do.

The courage to do this came from being very clear about my spiritual identity. In point of fact, I am neither male nor female. I am a soul, the child of God, currently inside a female form. I was also very clear about my aim, and concerned about how to be of more service to others.

The world has never looked to women for help in solving its problems. Instead it has turned to those of great authority, to scholars and to the very wealthy. This has been the crucial mistake.

The mother's role is to awaken the children with great love and prepare them for the rest of the day. She is their support. She nurtures.

Generally it is attachment to the home and children which prevent women from fulfilling their calling. To go beyond that attachment is no small accomplishment. To go beyond the fear of what society will say is no less.

My relationship with God gave me such internal power that I was not intimidated by social convention. The spirit was strong and so withstood all external pressures and influences.

Tolerance

There are three grades of tolerance:
to endure a situation, with a lot of obvious effort
to adapt and deal with a situation, using spiritual power
to pass right through it, not even noticing that something
needs tolerating

The sign of insufficient tolerance is: the minute someone says
any little thing, you start complaining or crying.
It doesn't seem right to be so sensitive

However, it isn't right to be insensitive either

Understand with love what other people are saying
Be sensitive to how others feel about what you say

Some are amazed that others take what they
say so badly. They say harsh things to others,
yet cannot tolerate being told anything themselves

Lack of tolerance creates impatience
which diminishes the spirituality,
the quality of love,
in the atmosphere

"How long do I have to go on like this?"
This is not using tolerance as a power
Remember, you are an actor on the stage of life
Step back. Play your part with detachment

Persevere in your spiritual efforts and
simply pass to the next grade!

Creating
Peace

Peace will be created by
coming face to face
with the things that are tearing
our human family apart

Greed, anger, ego,
attachment and lust
have destroyed peace
So there is too much sorrow in the world

It's not a question of going off
to remote places of quiet
or following a path that turns you
away from the world

It is a question of learning
'Humility'
And emerging humanity's
Mercy

Surrendering myself to God is the beginning
Together, we can then create peace.

Who Is God ?

The Heart Sees God

One of the first experiences I had on coming to this organisation, at its inception in the late 1930's, was feeling myself linked to God as if by a current of electricity. There was just this stream of electricity flowing directly from God to me. It was such an exhilarating experience that I knew that all I wanted to do was turn myself and my life over to God completely. Later, I began to feel as if God Himself had taken hold of my hand, and that it was He who was making me move forward. I still feel that way today. I feel His company constantly, and that the hand of His blessings is always on my head.

My experience is that you cannot see God with these physical eyes and you cannot understand God with a limited, gross intellect. Rather, God needs to be recognised, which is something far more revelatory than mere 'seeing' or philosophical understanding. 'Recognition' is not as much a matter of the physical brain as much as it is one of the heart. When the heart 'sees' God, when the heart 'knows' God, then there can be recognition. So recognition comes from feelings, experiences and understandings from the heart.

Recognising God

The first thing to recognise and understand is that God is One. He is unique; there can be no one but the one God alone who is called God. We need to understand that human beings are only human, that with humans there will be upheaval. The gods and goddesses of mythology and the idols and deities of the east were elevated beings, worthy of being worshipped, but who made them so elevated? It was God.

Understanding these things helped me to recognise God. Before coming to this organisation, I believed in God in a devotional way. This means that, although I had faith, there were no real, tangible experiences of who God was. Now my heart says: I have seen God, I know God. I have recognised God from the heart.

Touching and Understanding

Human beings believe that in order to understand they have to think. However, to understand God you don't have to think. When it comes to physical matters, then there's a need for thinking - you need to analyse, to figure a thing out. But not for God. Haven't you ever had a thought simply come to you 'out of the blue' - an intuition, or a sudden inspiration - without any actual thinking? God gave you that inspiration. Did you do any thinking? In one flash, God gave you that understanding. You didn't think, but suddenly the whole thing was clear to you, whereas under ordinary circumstances you wouldn't have got the picture even if you had thought about it for years.

God gave you that intuition.

He touched your intellect, your heart, like light.

It is truly a wondrous thing that God can touch us in this way, while He Himself is beyond thoughts. God does not think. God doesn't have the need to create any thoughts. And now He is making us like Himself - beyond wasteful and ordinary thoughts, beyond thought altogether. Actually, there is no need to think. Thinking too much is just a habit.

Companions of God

As our understanding and recognition of God grows, so does our love.
Yoga becomes an intense experience of being absorbed in love, lost in
that love. The effect is like that of fire - everything is transformed. In this
'fire of yoga' you are entirely consumed by the sweetness of God's
remembrance, and the experience of all relationships with Him. We are
made so clear and refined, there is the literal experience of becoming
angelic. This is the power of God's love for us. If God didn't love us, we
would never be able to achieve such heights.

I feel that God is doing so much for me personally. It is God's love which
is purifying me and filling me with spiritual might and mastery. It is His
love which has filled me with quietness and tranquillity. Because He is
always with me, I never feel alone. He is making us into angels,
the true companions of God.

Going Home

Here, in the corporeal world, everything is in constant motion.
The tides go in and go out. The sun rises and sets. Day turns into night
and night into day. However, in the Soul World, where God resides, all is
eternal, constant, stable and stationary. There are no changes whatsoever.

It is an experience of complete stillness.
It is beyond this world of five elements.

We leave the Soul World and take birth in a physical body, which is
made up of matter. The result is that we experience duality in life;
changes and contrasts such as sorrow and happiness and so on.
But God does not come into the cycle of birth and death and so in the
Soul World there is only stillness. As we learn to go to that Home and be
with God, we too become stabilised and still.

Becoming

God does so much, yet He is beyond the feeling of doing.
He does not think yet, still, you can say that He thinks.
That is His wonderful personality.
We cannot become God, because His part is unique.
But as His children, we can become like Him.
And this is all that God wants us to do.

The Inheritance

God is very happy to see us making the effort to become like Him. When we are not making this effort, He does not like it at all. This is because He is not just our Mother and Father, but He is our Teacher as well. A teacher is never happy when the students do not study well.

God has given us understanding, made us belong to Him and is sustaining us in such a way that we are becoming like Him. Of course there is a great difference between the Supreme Soul and other souls but, still, it is not difficult to become like Him. The more we can become like God and serve, the more we can become truly accurate instruments for His task. Then we can enjoy His company even more. God wants us to become like Him, and we want to become like God, so the desire of both parties is being fulfilled.

To become like the Father means that whatever qualities, virtues and powers God has, He gives them to us. They are given in the form of an inheritance. He feels that we are worthy and therefore He gives them as His inheritance. The virtues and powers that God gives us make it easy for us to become like Him. When we become like Him, then whatever He wants to do, He is able to do through us. So why should we not claim our inheritance from God? After all, He is not only God. He is our Father, too.

Knowledge and Power

We leave our original Home (the Soul World), come into this drama of life and eventually forget the plot. God never comes into the drama, and therefore does not ever forget the plot. So, He is the only One who can give us an understanding of the whole play. It is only God who possesses such knowledge; only He can come and give it. This is why He is the Supreme Soul. He is beyond, He is different; He is unique. He is the Father, and He gives us new life.

God is wonderful, you know. Even though He is not in the drama, He has the complete knowledge of the drama. He does not have to experience it to know it. He does not have eyes, but He sees our experiences. And He gives us recognition so that we can 'see' and know Him. Just as a generator sits in one place, continuously sending out an electric current, so the Almighty Father keeps sending us spiritual power. And we receive it - if, that is, we are linked properly and have taken care that no part has blown its fuse.

God's Role

God is the Director of the drama on this world stage, so He knows everything that's going on in the drama. In spite of this, it is not that He would just give the whole plot away. He tells us only that which it is necessary to know. As the Director, God helps us to understand this drama as it is, and to act accordingly. The drama moves along very slowly, so we should not hurry or worry. See the drama, understand it, and play your role. This is the training God gives us.

Previously we used to complain,
"Oh God, you are not listening to me; you are not helping me; you are not coming to me." Although it is true that God is the Director, He also has to act out His part according to the plot. This means that God cannot come even one second before His time in the drama.

God's role at this time in the drama is to enable us to have a relationship with Him. Being in His company in this way, I can be of help to God and thereby create my fortune. You start feeling the concern to play a good role in the drama, and to play it well, without laziness.

The End of the Search

Attraction to bodily names and forms has taken us away from God. This in turn has made us search for God, just as when someone has lost his beloved and he longs for her. Another example is a lost child. A child gets lost and is discovered by a stranger who tries to comfort him by offering everything. "Don't cry, honey, here is some candy, here are some toys." Yet in spite of all this attention, the child will still continue to cry. Why? Because he wants his mother. So why do we cry? We may have a good home, good parents, a good family, but still we cry because it is the soul that is lost, wanting the Mother, wanting the Father.

Once we find God, we stop crying. The search ends. This is why it is always said that the path of devotion is the path of reading scriptures, going on pilgrimages, searching for God. When God Himself comes, the search ends. And it is the same as when the mother appears in front of the child; whatever was given by the stranger is just thrown down, and the child runs to the mother. Whatever else had been given to the child, to distract him from his grief, is just thrown away when the mother is found.

So we can understand the plight of someone who is lost, the plight of a seeker. "Oh God, where are You? Do You really exist? When will that day come when I will meet You?" There are many such seekers whose thirst has not yet been quenched. Their desire still remains. This desperate state remains until God is recognised.

Influences

Let me be humble and
let me harmonise and work well with all others
But let me not become like them

Others may be influenced
by their own arrogance,
or by their own negativities,
or by ordinariness in the mind
But this does not mean that I have to be

There should be so much truth in me
that others become truthful

My inner state should be such that
not only am I not influenced
by the negativity of others
but my very presence is a positive influence
on all negativities
This is true, spiritual detachment

It is so exhilarating
to experience myself as a Spiritual Being
I should never hide it,
that sparkle on the face that comes
from having come to God

Everything I used to do on the basis of ego
can now be done out of love

Drama of Life
I

Every passing moment
is like a passing act in a play
We each of us are the Actors
playing our parts very well

An actor is never focused on another actor's part
Continually criticising it
He just gets on with his own part,
Playing it as best he can

This Drama of Life is eternal, predestined and accurate
Whatever anybody else says and does is their role
Not mine
My task is to play my part right

Right thoughts restore rightness to the whole play

Practise detaching yourself from your role
and experiencing the truth, behind the role
And you will find yourself loving
every instant of your role
And the Drama, too

And the question, "Why has this happened?"
will be answered

Drama of Life
II

Never have the thought that
you do not want a part
in the Drama of life

That is not possible

It is good to understand these things in detail
Understanding allows you to remove the sorrow,
makes you a self-sovereign,
And makes others this too

What is needed is to prepare the self internally
for whatever scenes may come
Attention to the self like this
removes all worry and concern

Then even extreme situations appear as side-scenes
They will come and they will go

Your mind will stay free, happy and powerful
And this is what you'll share with others

Drama of Life
III

The only thing we need to do is remember
"I am a soul and
around me is the Game of Life
playing itself out"

Then, whatever role comes up for me to play
I'll play it very well, no longer confusing
the Actor with the act

The one who remembers this is in God's eyes,
a hero. God says,
"Understand the part I have given you to play"

But though I do not see myself as God sees me
I should never say "How?"

God is the Director and He understands me very well
Realise this clearly
"God has understood me very, very well"

Helping God

The best way to ensure that we are a help to God is
to make sure we ourselves have taken
maximum help from God

He is not helped by our turning and asking Him
to please give help to a particular someone
God knows who needs help
He'll give it without our asking!

We help best by taking God's love and sharing it with others
and finishing our own complaints
There's danger in seeing the weaknesses of others
The mind tends to focus exclusively on that
just tiring itself out, being of benefit to no one

Spiritual love makes the mind work right
We want to help others see only the truth
Good wishes and love are always the first step to the solution
Loving our brothers and sisters is the solution

Mistakes

Expand your awareness a little and
mistakes no longer need make you feel guilty

For example, if you saw your life
as an Actor does his play
you would see one scene unfolding
after another

Each passing scene, having passed, is now over
Wisdom says: This is how to see it

Letting bygones be bygones is easier if you remember
You cannot change the past but you definitely can change the future
You can change, here and now, so that a mistake is not repeated
Connection with God gives you so much power
that your faults can be erased

Leading
Others

Good leadership is based on skills which are incognito
Like pure feelings, faith and trust
These keep both your frame of mind and the task
moving in the right direction

It is human to err, but your high hopes for someone
can actually eliminate errors
Doubting people has exactly the opposite effect

Believing in someone, extending feelings of trust
Never telling people what to do but
stepping aside and watching, with faith
This is what enables a task to get done in the right way

Spiritual skills like these are cultivated by
avoiding complacency, learning to be sensitive and staying alert
Keep an eye on your own spiritual health
Don't look to others for whatever is lacking, look within
See what remains to be done and do it
Never allow those with strong personalities to tell you what to do
especially when you feel something else to be right
This creates depression and you can't afford to be disheartened

Take care of yourself with understanding and love
making sure that you never compromise
your own spiritual growth

Being a Teacher

Teaching others is best done with subtlety
Explaining in such a way that the mind opens
because the heart has understood

Aim to inspire, rather than teach
My love for those I teach will do that
My love for God will do that
To the extent that I am soul conscious when teaching
so others will have this experience

Never force anyone to make spiritual effort
When the mind opens, this happens naturally
Avoid making comparisons
It creates loss of hope. Harbour no ill-will
And never try to score a point

Be like the parent
whose love for the child
is what's making him grow

Checking the Self

No matter how good a car or its driver,
if the car isn't regularly checked
there will be problems

In the same way,
If one moment I am happy, but in the next moment I'm not
Something is wrong
with the vehicle of my mind
And I will need to check it out

Check the smoothness of its flow
Is there purity? Has there been truth?
What about ego versus self-generated respect?
How much grief am I causing another?
Where are my weaknesses? How can I grow?

Checking these regularly and keeping them in shape
will deliver you to the destination

Carelessness in this will slow you down
Like getting stuck in a storm
You will feel yourself in a rut

So instead keep yourself tuned and ever-ready
Meditate at length, take power and love
Teach yourself how to be generous-spirited
And never stop giving

Introversion

Introversion comes with solitude,
the deep and silent company of God
which benefits the soul so profoundly

Introversion
creates that state of poise where
I think before I speak
I don't just speak
I can put my own nature aside
and easily avoid conflict with others

It does need practice
Like speaking only when necessary
And putting an end to excuses
about never having the time

With introversion, I can take charge of my mind,
purify the intellect and change any habit I want to
Spirituality takes root and I am transformed

Devotion and Wisdom

Devotional feelings are pure ones
consisting of sweetness and innocence
They are feelings of faith, in God
But they can be shaken

Faith, without some wisdom to back it up,
may fail you in a moment of need

Both are needed
for long-term spiritual attainment:
Like feeling close to God and close to others, too
in an unshakeable way
Or having true feelings, no matter what;
Becoming spiritually accomplished

If either faith or wisdom is lacking
your life cannot function right
It's like understanding your doctor's prescription
but somehow not trusting it anyway
It leaves you feeling unsure

So have a dialogue between your feelings and your understanding
They need to know each other, and work together, well!

The Intellect

The intellect is the vessel
which holds the knowledge of God.
It is different from the mind

A clean intellect is like the mind's filter
Sorting out thoughts of value from those of waste
Enabling me to put into action only
that which is of value
So much energy is saved in this way
Enabling me to do more, better and in less time

In India in the olden days, each household
kept a special vessel for water. The first thing
done, in the early morning hours of every day, was to
empty the vessel and put in fresh water

As the spiritual child of God,
the least I can do is
clean the vessel of my intellect
in the early morning hours of every day
And fill it with spiritual truths

Only when my intellect is clean and full
Will I then have something of value to offer others

Co-operation

Co-operation is based on four specific things.

First of all, constant pure feelings and elevated motives. If you aren't careful about cultivating the right kind of feelings in every moment, your nature will suffer.

Secondly, faith in God. Ego is cultivated when you don't understand that it is God who is doing everything. This ego creates competition and jealousy.

Thirdly, trust your colleagues and those who are close. This faith in others creates enthusiasm, which further serves to increase self-confidence.

Finally, communicate your motives constantly, using easy and simple language. This makes it possible for everyone to understand, and feel a part of the whole.

Newness

It is possible to become happy,
free, and deeply peaceful
And bring into your life the
literal, tangible companionship of God

These are extraordinary times
for reaching towards your highest ideals

Protection

If I don't know the enemy,
I will be poorly equipped to protect myself

Anger, greed, ego, lust, attachment are the enemy
in myself and in others
If I can't protect myself, who will?

Not to know the value of thoughts, or to move through
life without an aim, is ignorance
This is another kind of enemy.
To say: Things are okay as they are
means that I have not yet recognised my ignorance nor
my need for protection

The non-violent battle I have set out to win
is of overcoming the vices.
Spirituality
playing itself out as virtue and wisdom in my life
is my sword.
And my protection

Patience

The most important virtue needed for self-transformation
is Patience

Without Patience
you will lose hope in the transformation process

As you travel the path you sometimes run into rough spots
where the foot slips and you find yourself
suddenly not on the path, and there are
wrong thoughts or words or behaviour

Patience makes you cool and calm
It makes the journey possible

The process of self-realisation is not a ten yard dash
It is the one hundred and fifty mile run.
You have to learn to pace yourself

Patience teaches you to pace yourself

You can't take help from God until there is patience of this kind

Where there is patience there is peace
Where there is peace, there is love
This is a whole new experience of what it means to be human

Eternal Happiness

Eternal happiness comes when the mind and the senses have become quiet and peaceful. In that state, there is spiritual power: we are performing actions, but free from desires and free from attachment to what we do. Such happiness finishes any sorrow that may come to me. If anybody comes to me now with unhappiness, I am able to remove it so that the whole atmosphere around me becomes one of great peace. Yes, of course, this has taken time, but it has definitely happened.

Eternal happiness means the happiness that stays with me for ever, so that even if it feels as if it is running out I only need to reawaken the memory of it. Before I began these studies, I had reached a point in my life where happiness had disappeared, and I was filled with the desire to re-awaken it. And now today, that is where I am drawn to again and again; into that experience of eternal happiness.

Humility

Humility comes from understanding that the force behind whatever help you give to others comes not from you but from the power of love. It is not true that if you are humble others will walk all over you. It is when there is no humility that you can be easily influenced by others and things seem difficult. But when there is humility, there is also the power of truth. You know internally that you will achieve your aim, regardless of what others say or think. A humble person never feels they are bowing to others. The head is neither held high, nor lowered - just straight ahead, like an angel. Humility reveals your truth.

Ego makes you criticise others and get caught up in a web. Ego puts a lock on the intellect, obscuring your own responsibility: it says, "It is your fault, it has nothing to do with me." Humility is the key to this lock. It frees you from self-deception. Humility allows you to hear and obey your conscience. With humility there is the power of realisation, which allows transformation to take place. The soul can recognise a mistake in a second. It's easy to settle any argument easily -
"OK, I'm wrong..."

Humility makes the heart honest, big and clean. It enables you to be co-operative and have easy relationships with everyone. Humility enables you to win God's heart, the hearts of others and even your own heart! Inner conflict with your own feelings finishes, so confusion and difficulties also end. There is contentment, faith and the feeling of love for everyone.

Worry

Worry and sorrow come from remembering past relationships, possessions, or problems in the home or at work. It's as if these things exert a relentless influence over you - imprisoning you. Even if there has been a mistake, don't let the mind worry. Worrying prevents you from filling yourself with love from God. It is possible to fill the mind with so much love from God that there is no more room to add any worries. Eliminating worries in this way restores the strength of happiness.

Obstacles
Within

A major obstacle to spiritual progress is one's own negative nature. The root cause of this kind of nature is limited consciousness. This root has to be eliminated completely because obstacles that arise from a negative nature will prevent you from taking power from God.

Power from God is received through the awareness and faith that God belongs to you. A negative nature could destroy even this faith.

Recognising the root of the problem helps to transform it. Limited thinking should simply not be tolerated. There should be total cleanliness inside. For this you need to be very honest about the obstacles you are facing, because it is easy to deceive yourself. Limited thinking will be transformed when you spend time in the awareness of your true nature of peace and in being of help to others.

Changing Thoughts

Thoughts are like seeds. As are my thoughts, so will be my attitude and behaviour. Therefore my focus shouldn't be so much on wrong behaviour as on the thinking which causes it.

I need to be an aware of how much damage is caused by negative thoughts. Negative, wasteful thinking over a long period of time will put me right back into the gutter.

The task of a student of spirituality is to change situations through thoughts. I must change myself first, then I can change the world.

Early Morning Contemplation

The best time to dedicate to spiritual progress is the early morning
hours, whether for prayer, meditation or contemplation. Having rested
through the night, the intellect is fresh and pure. For expanding your
awareness, recognising God and taking a lot of spiritual benefit, four
o'clock in the morning is the best time. It's an invaluable time for
assessing ourselves and seeing how close we've come to self-realisation.
The signs of our progress or slackness are plainly visible. This
meditation reveals to us how much spiritual royalty
has been imbibed.

Spiritual Tolerance

Tolerance does not mean to simply leave a thing as it is - the "grin and bear it" attitude of the world. Spiritual tolerance enables you to stay within a crisis and help to resolve it, because tolerance is of a higher order, or higher power, than intolerance, ego, anger. It means you are able to respond with understanding, care and compassion to the situation. Where there are feelings of friendship and love, difficulties will be overcome. To tolerate something is a demonstration of goodwill, of having the aim to be co-operative and work for resolution.

Tolerance wins the hearts of others.

Strength

Spiritual strength is necessary if you want to grow spiritually and help others grow too. It's an inner kind of strength which builds character and allows you to discipline your mind.
A disciplined mind means a peaceful and happy one. A strong mind never gets disturbed.

To develop this strength, cultivate honesty and deep love and regard for God. This will allow you to protect yourself from being negatively influenced by your surroundings - both physical and emotional.

Blessings from others are another source of strength for the self. Blessings come to you from those you have served, and a very good way to serve others is to share this kind of inner strength. Those who have incorporated God's virtues in their outlook and activities are the ones who can give strength to others. To give guidance and wisdom like this means to give the lift of life.

Spiritual Medicine

The mind has an influence on the body and vice versa. These two work together, neither side can be ignored. Taking medicine is not wrong in principle; what is wrong is to attend only to the body and ignore the mind. If there is a need for medicine, then take it, but be careful that you don't let it be a support and become dependent.

When the mind is kept free from tension and worry, sleep comes naturally. Or, even if you can't sleep, there will be such peace and calm, you will still feel refreshed. Learn to be your own spiritual doctor. Whatever the nature of an illness - heart problems, cancer or simply intense pain - it is through the power of meditation, the remembrance of God, that illness can be overcome. This will also protect you from the negative things your friends and even doctors might say about your health.

Sometimes even just hearing about another's illness, people worry that they might have it and become ill as a result. If you have something wrong, to worry about it and spread your worry to others will only aggravate your ill-health. So even if the body is sick, learn how to let the mind simply remain in the remembrance of God.
If there is even a trace of worry, no cure can be effective.

Self-Awareness

A beautiful state of being is soul-consciousness, where your whole sense of self is shifted from a physical identity to a spiritual one. In soul-consciousness, you no longer feel yourself to be male or female, black or white. No worldly achievement forms your self-esteem. Instead, self-esteem is shaped by a deep, abiding experience of your intrinsic worth as a child of God.

A lack of soul-consciousness puts your well-being at the mercy of your environment - you become a slave to the influences of the people and situations around you - feeling happy and good only when outside events warrant it. This kind of dependency leaves the soul weak and confused. Soul-consciousness, on the other hand, frees you from external influences, allowing you to create an inner well-being which is totally independent.

Soul-consciousness is cultivated through deliberate practice and only those who have understood the need for this kind of true, inner, self-respect will make the effort. Difficulties will arise to test your resolve for self-upliftment - physical illness, relationships, memories of the past, and so on. Yet with patience and introspection, you will come to see how these very tests are the means to strengthen your spiritual identity.

Walking the Spiritual Path

We who walk the spiritual path are those who have enrolled ourselves in the school of spirituality. Our aim should be to pass all subjects, with honour. This means that spiritual understanding and power from God have been so well assimilated that not one of life's many challenges is faced without equanimity and truth. The heart is merciful and altruistic, never giving or taking sorrow. Feelings are pure, that is, devoid of any needs or expectations, and these pure feelings are shared abundantly with others. And we'll not have achieved this by becoming a hermit and leaving the world of everyday life; rather, we'll have remained completely in the world, yet distanced from all its vice and negativity.

Now is the time to become such a successful student of life; I should never doubt myself in this. Trust in God incurs His assistance. This plus my own determination will create the strength to move forward and progress. God is giving me everything. Have faith in this and proceed comfortably on the path to becoming like Him.

ABOUT THE BRAHMA KUMARIS
WORLD SPIRITUAL UNIVERSITY

The Brahma Kumaris World Spiritual University focuses on
understanding the self, its inner resources and strengths, and developing
attributes of leadership and the highest level of personal integrity.
With centres in 65 countries the University has, for the last 60 years
offered an education in human, moral and spiritual values.

As an international non-governmental organisation in consultative status
with the Economic and Social Council of the United Nations and
UNICEF, the University has organised three major international projects
during the last decade. These include 'The Million Minutes of Peace'
(1986), and 'Global Co-operation for a Better World' (1988 - 1991). The
most recent project 'Sharing Our Values for a Better World', launched in
1995, is dedicated to the 50th Anniversary of the United Nations.

Each of the University's 3000 centres worldwide offers the foundation
course in meditation and spiritual understanding, as well as lectures and
seminars on positive thinking, self management and stress management.
Courses and activities also take place in different areas of the community,
including hospitals, schools, prisons, business and industry.

All courses are offered free of charge, as a service to the community.

BRAHMA KUMARIS CENTRES
IN THE UNITED KINGDOM AND IRELAND

LONDON
Global Co-operation House, 65 Pound Lane, London NW10 2HH
Tel: 0181 459 1400 Fax: 0181 451 6480

NUNEHAM COURTENAY
Global Retreat Centre, Nuneham Park, Nuneham Courtenay,
Oxon OX44 9PG
Tel: 01865 343 551 Fax: 01865 343 576

EDINBURGH
20 Polwarth Crescent, Edinburgh, EH11 1HW
Tel: 0131 229 7220 Fax: 0131 229 7220

CARDIFF
15 Morlais Street, Roath Park, Cardiff, CF2 5HQ
Tel: 01222 480 557

DUBLIN, IRELAND
36 Lansdowne Road, Ballsbridge, Dublin 4, Ireland
Tel: (+353) 1 660 3967

WORLD HEADQUARTERS

Brahma Kumaris World Spiritual University
PO BOX NO.2, MOUNT ABU, RAJASTHAN 307501, INDIA

INTERNATIONAL COORDINATING OFFICE
AND EUROPEAN REGIONAL OFFICE
Global Co-operation House, 65 Pound Lane, London NW10 2HH, UK
Tel: (+44) 181 459 1400 Fax: (+44) 181 451 6480

REGIONAL OFFICES
AFRICA
PO Box 12349, Maua Close, off Parklands Road,
Nairobi, Kenya
Tel: (+254) 2 743 572 Fax: (+254) 2 743 885

AUSTRALIA AND SOUTH EAST ASIA
78 Alt Street, Ashfield, Sydney NSW 2131 Australia
Tel: (+61) 2 716 7066 Fax: (+61) 2 716 77 95

NORTH AND SOUTH AMERICAS
Global Harmony House, 46 S. Middle Neck Road,
Great Neck, NY 11021 USA
Tel: (+1) 516 773 0971 Fax: (+1) 516 773 0976

Your Local Contact is: